GREETINGS FROM OREGON

Mt. Hood at Twilight, Oregon

BY GIDEON BOSKER AND JONATHAN NICHOLAS

GRAPHIC ARTS CENTER PUBLISHING COMPANY

An Oregon Cherry Tree in Bloom.

International Standard Book Number: 0-932575-26-9
Library of Congress Catalog Number: 87-81347
Copyright © MCMLXXXVII Graphic Arts Center Publishing Company
P.O. Box 10306, Portland, OR 97210, 503/226-2402

Editor-in-Chief: Douglas A. Pfeiffer
Designer: Steve Bialer
Copy editor: Neil Anderson

Printed in the U.S.A.

FOREWORD

Upon first viewing this remarkable tribute to Oregon's cultural and scenic attractions, I was struck by the changes Oregon has undergone during the last century. Just as Celilo Falls disappeared years ago under the rising waters behind The Dalles Dam, many of the scenes depicted in these postcards no longer exist or have been radically altered.

Portland has transformed itself from the sleepy "Stumptown" of the 19th century into a vibrant, exciting urban center. Its waterfront now is accessible to people out for a stroll or a picnic, and many of the buildings seen in these cards are gone or dwarfed by newer structures. The magnificent Lewis and Clark Exposition, located in the northwest part of the city, exists only in pictures.

And important changes have occurred in Oregon's economy. As a former choker-setter for a logging operation, I particularly

enjoyed the scenes of our burgeoning timber industry in the early decades of this century. While the postcards portray our historic dependence on lumber, two new industries have vastly increased since World War II—electronics and tourism. Somehow, I don't think a postcard featuring a microchip will ever compete with the one of a family living inside a tree stump.

The busy salmon cannery at Astoria, the amusement rides on Council Crest, passenger trains to the coast, the majestic Portland Hotel—all these are memories to us now, forever preserved in these pages.

But after noting the obvious differences between then and now, I realized there is much here that is reassuringly familiar. The scenic splendors depicted in the book remain largely unchanged because thousands of Oregonians have fought to preserve and protect them for future generations. The Public Beaches Law, the Scenic Rivers Act, the Bottle Bill and recent efforts to protect the Columbia River Gorge, all testify to the fact that Oregonians are wise stewards of our land, air, ocean, rivers and streams.

Think of these postcards as messages from the past, telling us that something less tangible than scenery still endures—the indomitable spirit of Oregonians.

These pictures show a continuity with the past, yet we know how different our world is from that of our forebears. I wonder what cultural artifacts will remain in 50 or 100 years to remind our children and grandchildren, as these postcards remind us, of our qualities as Oregonians? What will remain to demonstrate our high regard for our natural resources, to show how we worked and how we played?

Like me, I'm sure that many of you will wonder what messages were written on the other sides of these cards. What did the senders write to their friends and loved ones about themselves, their experiences, their state? I'd like to think it was something like this: "Having a wonderful time—there is no place on Earth quite like Oregon."

GOV. NEIL GOLDSCHMIDT

A panoramic view of Albany.

*Dedicated to Thelma Bengs, whose love of
postcards and of Oregon knows no bounds.*

CONTENTS

INTRODUCTION

From the time they were first produced in Europe during the 1860s, postcards have painted idealized pictures of the scenes that inspired them. Fulfilling the desire of wandering adventurers to bring the exotic close to home, these inexpensive souvenirs projected an unrivaled pride of place. They made it possible for travelers to communicate the beauty, the human interest and the sheer majesty of what they were experiencing to those far away.

In Oregon, there never has been a shortage of people, places or activities to celebrate. There emerged in the region a dedicated cadre of postcard photographers who recorded it all, from the refined, marble-walled interiors of Portland's Parisian-inspired pastry shops to the rolling golden wheatlands of huge ranches near Pendleton.

The first souvenir postcard in America was produced for the World's Columbian Exposition held in Chicago in 1893. Postcards began to appear in Oregon around 1900, and nearly all were commissioned by out-of-state publishers such as Edward H. Mitchell of San Francisco; Emil Pinkau of Leipzig, Germany; and Raphael Tuck & Sons of London. Most of the scenes on these cards were photographed by such celebrated Oregon photo-

1006—AGATE BEACH, OREGON COAST HIGHWAY

graphers as Wesley Andrews, Joseph Buchtel, Frank G. Abell and Peter Britt.

Cards based on their work usually were printed by German lithographers and then shipped back to the United States for distribution through a network of importers and jobbers. Picture postcards published by Oregon companies—most notable among them, the Portland Postcard Company, B.B. Rich, Louis Scheiner Co., Chas. Lipshuetz Co., E.E. Lavalleur and others—began to appear in 1904. Postcard publishing during this era reached its zenith during the Lewis and Clark Exposition of 1905. Portland mailboxes must have bulged beneath the onslaught of more than 450 different cards printed for this event featuring the fair's astonishing assortment of buildings, "gayways" and scenic attractions.

However talented were Oregon's practitioners of the photographic arts, their images provided only a "rough sketch" for the final printed card. It was then up to the lithographer to fill in the rudimentary black-and-white image with retina-searing inks that issued from the printing press or, on occasion, for illustrators to hand-tint cards with watercolors or oil pigments.

Not surprisingly, then, the visual chronicle that follows is remarkable in its beauty and in its range. Using picture postcards, we have attempted to illustrate the story of a region whose inhabitants have many faces and occupations, whose cities stimulate the eye in countless ways, and whose varied landscapes create countless moods and rhythms. Culled primarily from the Thelma Bengs Collection, a private holding of more than 25,000 Oregon postcards, these images depict a state populated by men and women—both rural and urban—who have had the resourcefulness and the imagination to harness the best of what their land had to offer.

Each postcard can be viewed as a frame in an imaginary silent movie that tells a story of natural beauty, human conquest, industry and recreation, all coexisting in a state dotted with an eclectic mix of settlements from dense urban pockets and lamplit lumber ports to mist-shrouded fishing villages and solitudinous towns where booted and spurred men still ride.

From the refined architecture of its cities to the serene vistas and overpowering landscapes that are part of its natural heritage, Oregon is a diverse, even mysterious land. The region owes its distinctiveness to a period of intense vulcanism that hurtled great peaks of crystalline sharpness through the ooze and miasma of prehistoric time. If the state was cleaved physically by the Casacade Mountain range, it was divided metaphysically by economic, political and sociological barriers of much greater magnitude. The dry country of Eastern Oregon, with its droughts, distances and high desert sparsely mottled with stunted juniper and wind-sculpted sage, turned its inhabitants into cattlemen and sheepherders just as more fertile circumstances molded residents west of the mountains into loggers, fishermen and fruit farmers. And its urban centers made them into architects and attorneys, bankers and builders, fashion designers and financiers. These geographic variations guarantee that there never will be any such thing as a typical Oregonian.

In this light, we have selected images that paint a balanced picture of Oregon—both of its land and of its people. What emerges is a rich composite of pastoral scenes and well-groomed cities; bucolic landscapes and busy downtowns. Here are heartfelt scenes of a people who pried open the doorway to the unknown West, found a tough job to do and then did it with unprecedented purpose of vision.

G.B. AND J.N.

THE MIGHTY COLUMBIA

There is no mystery to the allure of the great gash, the sylvan slash, that the Columbia River carves through the Cascades in its headlong rush from heartland to sea. Wrapped in mist, lashed by wind, cooled by shadow, bathed in moonlight, the Columbia Gorge in all its guises extends a vicelike grip on our emotions, our climate and our economy. From the magnificent vantage of Crown Point, in a single, slow sweep of the gaze, one can drink deep of all the munificence of Oregon.

Since pioneers first explored the region, the river has exerted an inexorable pull on those who drew close to it. In the 16th century, seafarers rounding the Horn, probing ever farther northward in search of the fabled Northwest Passage, traded not only in piracy and pelts, but in rumors of a great river of the West. Yet for 200 years the mouth of the river eluded them. Not until the morning of May 11, 1792, did Captain Robert Gray, sailing out of Boston in the Columbia Rediviva, finally settle the matter once and for all. Bravely ordering sails hoisted, he steered a treacherous course through the seething breakers of the bar and entered the Oregon country. The great river of the West would lie hidden no longer.

679 — Mouth of the Columbia River, Oregon.

In those early days of exploration, the arrival of each tall ship was greeted by scores of canoes, their inhabitants scurrying forth to engage in barter. Sea otter skins traded hands for trinkets. And when seamen later learned that these furs, in which they held little interest, commanded a king's ransom in China, the race for control of the Northwest was on.

To this day, tiny vessels rush forth from land to greet visitors from afar. But these boats that race from shore bear not pelts but river pilots, the men who ride shotgun on ocean-going vessels as they nudge their way up the narrow, meticulously maintained channel into port. Where fearless trappers once rode roaring rapids and heavily laden sternwheelers steamed to and fro, squat-nosed tugboats now growl, easing forward elephantine barges tied trunk to tail. And the centuries old trade of buffalo skins for basketwork between native tribes of the interior and the coast has been supplanted by a more modern exchange: soft white wheat for Toyotas.

But the river is much more than a mode of transportation or vital artery for commerce. It is a canvas upon which Mother Nature paints her many moods, using brushstrokes broad and gentle. In its higher reaches, with adolescent impetuosity, the Columbia tumbles precipitously from a pristine Canadian lake, coursing through canyons as if impatient to flee forests of cedar and fir. In its middle passage, a more composed and mature river meanders across the desert landscape. Here it does double duty, providing both water for irrigation and power to pump it to thirsting crops. Finally, in its lower reaches, the Columbia is wide, slow and stubborn. It hides in backwaters and eddies, as if reluctant to mcct its destination in the pounding of the surf.

More than 1,200 miles the Columbia flows, draining a territory of 259,000 square miles. But the heart of the river lies in that 50-mile stretch from The Dalles to the mouth of the Sandy River. Here, framed by towering basalt cliffs, buffeted by winds that cross a continent, tinted by a thousand shades of green, lies a gorge unlike any other. A gorge that is free, fecund, wild. And hidden beneath the surface of its waters, fighting against the flow, run silver salmon. Year after year, they return to test their primeval urging against all obstacles men set in their path. Still deeper circle the Columbia's oldest inhabitants, the sturgeon, bearers of a secret to survival that man may never know.

363. VISTA HOUSE, COLUMBIA RIVER HIGHWAY, ORE.

©Weister Co. Portland, Ore.

With tireless tempest and commanding calm, the Columbia registers the changing seasons of the Pacific Northwest. In January it can glisten, locked in the crystalline embrace of a silver thaw, while in April, swollen waterfalls tumble like so many necklaces from the jewel box skyline. In June, when soft sunlight dances upon the water, it summons bathers to its shallows. And in August, when hikers seek out the shadows of its countless canyons, moss and fern provide cool refuge from the womb of summer. But no matter what the season, over one's shoulder there always stands some silent sentinel, some massive outcropping, some oblique statuary of rock cloaked in lichen and etched by time.

Through all this visual splendor winds engineer Samuel Lancaster's asphalt legacy, a highway of poetry and drama. For some, this road, on which millions travel each year, provides proof positive that the gorge has been "tamed." Dams may indeed have caused this mighty river to pool, to deepen and to wait. But let no man think the Columbia, harnessed by steel and concrete, has bowed to his bidding. Come one moonless night to its shallows, and hear its waters singing. Rivers bend but do not break.

OREGON, Indians at Home on the Columbia River.

OREGON, Fish Trap on the Columbia River.

Picturesque Scenery on Beautiful Columbia River.

2287 — SEINING FOR SALMON, COLUMBIA RIVER, OREGON.

314. CASTLE ROCK, SEEN FROM THE COLUMBIA RIVER HIGHWAY.

Rooster Rock, Columbia River, Oregon.

PUBLISHED BY B.B. RICH, OFFICIAL STATIONER.

Cascade Locks.

Willamette Falls.

PUBLISHED BY B.B. RICH, OFFICIAL STATIONER.

Bishop Cap at Shepperd's Dell,
Columbia River Highway, Oregon

In 1896 the federal government built a series of locks around the treacherous Casades Rapids. Although skilled Indians and French-Canadian boatmen were sometimes able to negotiate the rapids, it was customary for even the most daring to disembark and portage their cargoes.

OREGON, Celilo Falls, Columbia River.

Fish Wheel and Indians Snagging Salmon at Celilo Falls on Columbia River, Oregon 13

(C) Cross & Dimmitt

Indians have Perpetual Fishing Rights at the Falls.

INDIANS FISHING AT CELILO FALLS
OF COLUMBA RIVER IN OREGON—P54

*Drowned by rising waters behind The Dalles Dam, Celilo Falls was a fishing
station held by the Indians under a treaty granting them exclusive and perpetual
fishing rights. Long before Lewis and Clark passed through the area, fishing
stands were handed down from father to son.*

1462- Log Raft on the Columbia River, Oregon. On Line of O.W.R.&N.Co.

1464- Seining for Salmon, Columbia River, Oregon.

Tugboats, the great workhorses of the Columbia River, still dutifully herd the rafts of logs that float from forest to mill. In earlier days, stout ponies helped pull seines, large fishing nets with floats along the top edge and weights along the bottom.

169:—MULTNOMAH FALLS, COLUMBIA RIVER HIGHWAY, ORE.

Multnomah Falls.

Dear Sis Please write all the news wright away your Sophia P.

PUBLISHED BY B. B. RICH, OFFICIAL STATIONER.

Multnomah Falls, Columbia River.

With its source some 4000 feet above the highway near the summit of Larch Mountain, Multnomah Falls drops 680 feet into a tree-lined basin. This natural wonder inspired Samuel Lancaster, builder of The Columbia Highway, to write: "There are higher waterfalls and falls of greater volume, but there are none more beautiful than Multnomah."

VISTA HOUSE, CROWN POINT,
COLUMBIA RIVER HIGHWAY, OREGON

Columbia Gorge Hotel, Finest Hotel on Columbia River Highway,
2 Miles West of Hood River, Ore.

10

194. "PACIFIC HIGHWAY INTERSTATE BRIDGE," SPANNING COLUMBIA RIVER, PORTLAND, ORE. TO VANCOUVER, WASH.

BONNEVILLE DAM
CONNECTING WASHINGTON WITH OREGON

*Designed in 1918 by architect Edgar M. Lazarus, the Vista House was Oregon's first example of Art Nouveau architecture. The copper-domed structure features expansive arched windows set into walls faced with rough ashlar sandstone.
In 1921, Portland architect Morris Whitehouse used an Italian scheme for the Columbia Gorge Hotel. Set on a high bluff overlooking the Columbia, the hotel was executed in white stucco and red tile used in beachside Italian hostelries.*

The Columbia River Gorge is one of the most beautiful areas in the Pacific Northwest, if not in all of North America. One can imagine the awe of Meriwether Lewis and William Clark when they first viewed this scenic wonder during their westward expedition in 1805. The Gorge is the only navigable passage through the Cascade Mountains, and contains spectacular vistas and unique combinations of climate, vegetation, and landforms. The west end is a land of waterfalls and lush rain forests. The eastern portion opens into oaks and grasslands, and finally blends into the sagebrush and open spaces for which much of the West is known.

During the 11,000 years of human activity in the Columbia River Gorge, its beauty and grandeur have impressed those who live and visit there. I wish everyone could stand on Crown Point and view the Gorge, and see what a unique creation God has given us.

— SEN. MARK O. HATFIELD

310. COLUMBIA RIVER HIGHWAY BETWEEN MULTNOMAH FALLS AND ONEONTA GORGE.

323. WINDOWS IN MITCHELL'S POINT TUNNEL, COLUMBIA RIVER HIGHWAY, OREGON.

BRIDGE OF THE GODS, "ON THE COLUMBIA RIVER HIGHWAY"   14

7629. Excursion Steamer "Dalles City" leaving Cascade Rapids, Columbia River, Oregon.

THE "BAILEY GATZERT," IN THE RAPIDS, NEAR CASCADE LOCKS.

SEEN FROM THE COLUMBIA RIVER HIGHWAY.

311. CAPE HORN AND CIGAR ROCK.

241. ONEONTA GORGE, COLUMBIA RIVER HIGHWAY, ORE.

243. ONEONTA BLUFFS ON THE COLUMBIA RIVER, OREGON.

246. THUMB NEEDLE, COLUMBIA RIVER, ORE.

ONE OF THE OBJECTS OF INTEREST TO TRAVELLERS

240. ST. PETER'S DOME, ON THE COLUMBIA RIVER.

245. ROOSTER ROCK ON THE COLUMBIA RIVER, ORE.

With their dramatic sculpting, the bluffs lining the Columbia River are among the most interesting geologic formations in the region. Many are sheer-walled canyons that once lined old Indian burial grounds and inspired many legends about the area. Oneanta Gorge is a deep narrow cleft in a basalt bluff where fossilized trees have been caught in its perpendicular walls. Just east of Horsetail Falls towers is St. Peter's Dome, a 2,000 foot basalt pinnacle. Rooster Rock overlooks a popular fishing and swimming hole.

IN HIGH PLACES

From the precipitous faces of the wild Wallowas to the tumbling folds of the snow-capped Sisters, the Oregon high country is etched with ranges where spring-fed lakes are slung like hammocks between chiseled faces of obsidian sharpness. A cordillera of volcanic peaks running north and south, the Cascades divide the state into a marine western portion and a continental eastern portion. They are directly responsible for the striking differences in climate and geography that characterize each region. But this is only part of the story. However conspicuous they may be, these majestic cones thrusting into blue shuttles of sky are but fragments of a much more complex dialogue between earth, water and stone.

Deeply hidden in the gothic forests of these slopes is a never-ending symphony of falling water, what some call "Oregon's unofficial state song." Smooth, deep currents, cascades and eddies sing around every spruce tree and pinecone, coursing over moss-mottled rocks that have been worn to bulbuous smoothness by the toil of time. On their way to the mighty Columbia, these fountains bloom white in falls, glide in crystal plumes, surge gray and foam-filled through boulder-choked gorges and then quietly slip

from the woods in long, tranquil streams. One can hear these waters "chanting all together in one grand anthem," explained the celebrated naturalist John Muir, "and comprehend them all in clear vision, covering the range with white lace."

Nowhere has this relentless anthem of stone, tree and cascading water become familiar to more Oregonians than on Mount Hood, one of the lordly sentinels of the Cascade Range that extends from California into Alaska. Proud and glorious with its razor-sharp peak, the mountain has been an omnipresent reminder of pioneer values and has been held in high esteem since its slopes and trails were first colonized by public enthusiasts in the mid-1920s. "I am a native son of Oregon...and yield to no one in sentimental regard to Mount Hood," wrote John A. Lee, a Mazama member in 1927. "It is one of the noblest and most beautiful of our mountains and its historic associations I value highly."

With its jagged backbone and creamy crown, Wy'east, as the Klickitat Indians called it, has long been viewed by Oregonians as a place for spiritual and physical invigoration, and as an antidote to the urban ills and tensions that taint city life even in outposts as remote as Portland. For more than 60 years, arduous conditions on the glacial peak have attracted a hardy breed of mountaineers who have recreated on its silky slopes in pursuit of self-sufficiency and adventure. This cadre of trekkers and skiers, declared Richard Montague in a speech delivered before the Mazamas, makes the pilgrimage to Mount Hood to feel "the stirrings of ancestral instinct, harking back to the time when those surroundings of hill and heather …were the theater of our joys and sorrows, the scene and setting of human life."

"One and one-half hours from roses to snow," is the way many old-timers describe the 63-mile journey from Portland to Timberline Lodge, Oregon's 50-year old alpine refuge anchored on the southwestern slope of Mt. Hood. A million-dollar resort in a million acre playground, Timberline is host to thousands of people each year. The four-story stone and wood structure, replete with handcrafted furnishings produced in the 1930s under the auspices of the WPA, is located a short distance from the old Barlow Pass where Oregon's pioneers first "looked over the rim of the long trail to their promised land."

Very different but equally dramatic in sheer physical beauty is Crater Lake, the calderic remnant of a pre-historic mountain–later named Mount Mazama–that collapsed into an empty magma chamber about 6,600 years ago. Whether one gazes upon this surreal landscape from the vantage of an armchair geologist or captivated tourist, it is impossible not to be entranced by the constant dance of light and shadow against lichen-colored palisades, by the pools of water alternating between Prussian blue and turquoise, and by the variety of wild-flowers–bleeding hearts, paintbrush and Lewis Monkeyflower–dotting trails that ascend to the summit of 8,926-foot Mount Scott.

From North Sister peak to Chief Joseph Mountain, the Oregon high-lands offer mere mortals the opportunity to stand atop great pinnacles and grapple with Nature in her wildest moods. As Warren D. Smith, professor of geology and geography at the University of Oregon once wrote, "You who have stood amidst the crackle of electricity on the lonely mountain top, you who looked into the bowels of an ice stream, you who have gazed into the yawning hissing throat of a volcano, you who have listened to the silence of the night in the fir forest or far above the snowline, you have indeed a 'sense of deeper things.'"

3277- Mt. Hood, Oregon.

THE SUMMIT OF MT. HOOD, OREGON.

Early development of Timberline Lodge pitted devout preservationists who warned against invasion by a "coarse unenlightened public," against civic groups who claimed that new facilities on the glacial behemoth were essential for delivering the region from obscurity. In the end, Timberline proved that a public project could both honor the lofty sentiments of pioneers and embrace the public's pent-up desire to participate in recreational pursuits.

167:—TOP OF MT. HOOD, SHOWING RANGER'S CABIN, ORE.

Timber Line Lodge, Mt. Hood National Forest, Oregon. Altitude 6000 Feet

15-628 Timberline Lodge and Mt. Hood - Government Camp, Oregon

Mt. Hood, Oregon.

15-811 Main Lounge - Timberline Lodge - Gov't. Camp, Oregon

15-595 Ski Lounge - Timberline Lodge - Government Camp, Oregon

17-178 Mt. Hood Skiway from Upper Terminal

15-812 Bed Room Suite - Timberline Lodge - Gov't. Camp, Oregon

15-901 Coffee Shop - Timberline Lodge, Oregon

M-502 Corner of the Dining Room - Battle Axe Inn - Government Camp, Ore.

M-615 Fountain and Lunch Counter, Battle Axe Inn - Government Camp, Ore.

917 - MT. HOOD FROM PORTLAND, OREGON.

OREGON, Mt. Hood.

Mt. Hood, Oregon. Hood River Valley in Foreground

12

Mt. Hood, as seen from near the Peninsula. Oregon.

155:—Sunset on Mt. Hood, Oregon.

168:—REFLECTION LAKE, NEAR GOVERNMENT CAMP, MT. HOOD LOOP, ORE.

MOUNT HOOD FROM LOST LAKE,
SHOWING WATER REFLECTION.
"THE PARADISE OF OREGON"

Beautiful Mt. Hood, Portland, Oregon

30

Alone, and then alone again, the summits
go on, lost by the course they lead,
like a lake or an ocean alone just once,
too big to have a friend.

Then here all at once in the meadow grass, fieldmice
rustle soft, such deep company, so near a glimpse,
that we face the snow possessed, at home in such
chance things hidden around—

Warm places the giants left.

— WILLIAM STAFFORD

Beautiful Mt. Hood, Oregon, showing Auto Road.

Mt. Hood from Lost Lake, Oregon

70 – Mt. Hood, Oregon. Elevation 11225 Feet.
ON LINE OF O-W. R. & N. CO.

Cloud Cap Inn & Summit of Mount Hood, Ore.
Elevation of Inn, 7000 ft.

The seed for Timberline Lodge, Cloud Cap Inn was a small hostelry that stood on the mountain's north slope since 1889. This charming architectural structure boasted majestic views of the mountain's craggy summit on one side and the verdant Hood River Valley on the other. The inn never really thrived, nor could its eight guest rooms accomodate the vast hordes of tourists who began to visit the mountain by the mid-1920s.

D 12 Wallowa Lake, near Joseph, Oregon

Mt. Jefferson and Hanging Valley, Oregon

Copyright, 1907

D 8 Alder Slope, from Enterprise, Ore.

Cradled in the crater of an extinct volcano, and walled by majestic cliffs, the miraculously blue Crater Lake has been named with Grand Canyon and Victoria Falls as one of the three scenic marvels in the world. Perched on an extraordinary viewpoint on the south end of the lake, Crater Lake Lodge is a three-story hotel located near Rim Village.

3074 – The Three Sisters, Oregon.

THE DRY COUNTRY

Winter's dawn comes hard to the high desert. An hour before first light, the wind steals down from the Strawberry Mountains, and a temperature 50 degrees below zero tightens like a belt on the town of Seneca, population 208. On the broad open range, steers turn their backs on sprawling acres and huddle together as if seeking to share the warmth of their shallow breathing. On some distant rimrock, a choir of coyotes harmonizes an homage to the darkness. Nothing moves save the sliver of a moon. As the sun peeks over the distant horizon, an endless ocean of sagebrush takes on a soft gray glow. Shadows start their daylong dance from fenceposts; dogs chase impatience and their tails. Soon the first rustlings are heard in the ranchhouse. Warm feet are thrust into cold boots. A match strikes; a fire crackles. Horses grow restless in the barn.

Oregon's high desert is vast: 24,000 square miles. But miles don't count for much in the dry country. Reub Long, cowboy chronicler of these parts, liked to say you don't measure desert distance by miles, but by looks. According to Reub, the Oregon desert is 10 good looks across. At first "look," then, the dry country can

Cattle on The Desert near Paisley Central Oregon.

seem a hopelessly inhospitable place, a seamless expanse of emptiness, an endless web of dust and broken dreams. But something about its stubbornness, its serenity and sheer sense of space, reaches out to certain men and grabs them. The desert holds them and–sometimes forever–locks them in its spell.

Traces have been found of cave dwellers who lived in Eastern Oregon more than 10,000 years ago. The first white men to explore the region were fur traders and trappers–the emissaries from the Hudson's Bay Company. No desert lovers were they. On the track of their elusive quarry, they crept along the creek beds, skulking from tree to lonely tree. Later came the miners, men hellbent on catapulting themselves from priva-tion to princely fortune. Hungry for gold, they fed most frequently on frustration. Next arrived sheepherders, the loneliest of men, tending their vast roaming flocks. Ceaselessly they skirmished with their arch enemies, cattle barons who, in the manner of medieval lords, ruled over vast estates and dust-caked buckaroos.

In the early years, desert land was offered free to settlers. There were few takers. And of those few, fewer still survived. Oregon's great grass sage, E.R. Jackman,

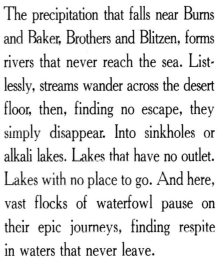

wraps up half a decade of struggle between man and nature in a sentence: "It usually took five years for a man to arrive, build a house, fence some land, break it, put in a crop, wait in vain to harvest it, lose his money, get tired of jackrabbit stew, and leave." Despite these hardships, to those who linger in its lure there is an uncanny beauty to the Oregon desert. And a timelessness. Eastern Oregon is the sort of place where a man finds himself stopping whatever he's doing, and then just standing there awhile, gazing, drinking in the emptiness.

There's lots of emptiness to drink. There are more elk than people in Wallowa County. Lots more. The people like it that way. So, most likely, do the elk. Sometimes called "The Switzerland of Oregon," the Wallowas stand guard over a richly varied landscape that ranges from the pristine isolation of the Eagle Cap Wilderness to the plunging chasm of the Snake River Gorge. This is a land where stark soaring peaks, mile-high lakes and flower-splashed meadows overlook a sparsely-peopled sea of broken rimrock and bare plain. The desert's southern boundary, too, is marked by the massive lonely bulk of mountains. The huge monolith of Steens Mountain bursts like an uninvited guest into the family of the desert floor. Its

Main Street, Pendleton, Ore.

crest, creased by ferocious lightening storms and dusted by summer snows, is sliced by huge gorges, verdant fissures that seem to plunge into the bowels of the earth. Over these great gaping wounds, eagles soar, and meadowlarks sing.

The dry country holds many mysteries, perhaps, none more elusive than its rain. The precipitation that falls near Burns and Baker, Brothers and Blitzen, forms rivers that never reach the sea. Listlessly, streams wander across the desert floor, then, finding no escape, they simply disappear. Into sinkholes or alkali lakes. Lakes that have no outlet. Lakes with no place to go. And here, vast flocks of waterfowl pause on their epic journeys, finding respite in waters that never leave.

But beyond the beauty, beyond the bobcats and badgers and the reach-out-and-touch-them stars, there is something else mighty about the Oregon desert: its stillness. A stillness that sneaks up on men and that is never far away. This quietude is both the strength and the terror of the Oregon desert. In the final analysis, though they'd never admit it, this is most likely why its residents remain. The dry country is the easiest place in Oregon for a man to be alone with himself and his maker. And that makes it an awfully hard place to leave.

908   GRAND CANYON OF THE SNAKE RIVER, WORLD'S DEEPEST GORGE

BOUNDARY LINE BETWEEN IDAHO AND OREGON

PHOTO BY WESLEY ANDREWS

392.   HELL'S SMOKE STACKS, ONE OF THE WONDERS OF OREGON'S SCENERY.

© Weister Co.

Shearing Sheep, Eastern Oregon.

Modern Harvesting
Near Pendleton, Ore.

The undulating Snake River, with a sculpted gorge wider and deeper than the Grand Canyon, forms more than half the eastern boundary of the state. Hell's Smoke Stacks, part of the Seven Devils Range, is characteristic of the unusual erosion formations created by lava flows in the region.

LITTLE INDIAN CHIEF, UMATILLA TRIBE, PENDLETON, OREGON

In the early years of the nineteenth century, there were estimated to be 1500 Umatillas living in northeast Oregon. By 1923, the tribe's population had fallen to 145. In 1962, one report suggested that as few as ten remained.

Chief Yu — ma — sum — Kin (Grizzley Shirt) Cayuse Tribe, Oregon.

An Eastern Oregon Sheep Range.

78. Adam's Ave, La Grande, Oregon.

Wheat awaiting shipment, Eastern Oregon.

Wheat in an Oregon Warehouse.

Photo only copyrighted 1907 by Kiser Photo Co., Portland, Ore.

"Bronco-Busting" on an Oregon Cattle Ranch.

St. Elizabeth Hospital, Catholic Cathedral, and St. Francis Academy, Baker City, Ore.

Harvesting an Eastern Oregon Grain Crop, near Baker City, Ore.

Steam Combine, Eastern Oregon.

Among the most unusual postcards depicting Oregon scenes are these hand-colored gelatin cards, which look like miniature paintings in a frame.

In the slow ascent from the shades of green and azure, up from eddying surf and sand, through the fruitful web of western river valleys, the Oregon traveler breasts the Cascade crest. At last astride those jagged spines of alpine travail, every lateral view to the east reveals a canvas of grey, tawny, ochre, granite, and sage as golden buckskin highlights puma and palomino shadows.

Unknowing eyes perceive an undulating iron-hard sameness where all is alike—acres, sections and townships. Yet they are as different as icy winter on hoary summits and the fierce orange summer days when the reynard yellow sun strikes the high desert anvil. Those arid wastes far above deep canyons enfold heavy alfalfa fields, stout homes and secret groves of groaning peach trees fed by the cold water of trout-choked streams.

Nature reigns, as always—her winds tirelessly scouring scarred northern slopes, dry gulches and the eroded posts of scrawny farmsteads left so long ago to an elementary, cruel, unforgiving, parching force that, for an hour, can be so suddenly heady and sublime. The buttes, the rimrock, the shale land of peregrines, pronghorns, laughing chukars and doleful coyotes, and the horny-handed men evoke a way of Oregon life spent ten thousand years before Rome. This silent, star-jammed vaulted landscape now and again finds its own time to make its dogged statement.

—THOMAS VAUGHAN

Harvesting Scene.

Street Scene, Bend, Ore.

STREET SCENE, BEND, OREGON

PETERSON'S ROCK GARDEN, BEND AND REDMOND, OREGON

GOD BLESS AMERICA

PETERSEN'S ROCK GARDEN, BEND AND REDMOND, OREGON

Petersen's Rock Garden first sprouted as the outgrowth of the hobby of a Danish immigrant farmer living six miles north of Tumalo. It eventually grew into a fairytale landscape of houses, churches, castles, bridges, lagoons, — even the Statue of Liberty — all crafted from native rock.

Modern Saw Mill, La Grande, Oregon.

Beet Sugar Factory, La Grande, Oregon.

FOSSIL ROCKS, JOHN DAY HIGHWAY, OREGON—P155

JEWEL ON THE WILLAMETTE

Inspiration for Portland's development into a metropolis with great architectural aspirations can be traced to words Albert E. Doyle penned while on his deathbed: "Wanting something is the first process in getting it," wrote the Portland architect. "Sooner or later, we all put concrete foundations under our air castles." Since the city's beginnings more than a century ago, its builders, architects and citizens have been unusually self-conscious about the look of their emerging metropolis. Boasting Beaux-Arts office buildings shimmering with terra cotta skins, cast-iron facades with the visual rhythms of Venetian arcades, and controversial experiments in Postmodernism, Portland makes it possible to assimilate almost the entire history of American architecture within the province of a short promenade.

Portland's tradition in urban architecture can be traced back to the smell of foundry fumes and the clang-jangle of iron ingots being stripped of their molds–to the urging sounds of steel mills that produced components for the city's first commercial buildings. Portland's "Venice by the Willamette," a clustering of cast-iron architecture bursting with exuberant ornamentation, sprang up along the riverfront between 1853 and 1889. After the San Francisco earthquake, the city could lay claim to the largest collection of such structures west of New York City's SoHo district. Stylistically unified and packed like sardines along Front and First, the iron-fronted jewels of Warren H. Williams, Justus Krumbein and others, cast a treasury of shadows along Portland's bustling, shop-lined streets.

The first glimmer of Portland's architectural prowess came to light in 1881, when Henry Villard of the Pacific Terminal Company recruited America's most acclaimed architectural firm, McKim, Mead and White of New York City, to design and oversee construction of the Portland Hotel. Unwittingly, the railroad baron kindled a white-hot tradition that, during the next century, would enrich the city with buildings, parks and fountains reflecting the most enlightened architectural thinking of the times. During this period, such esteemed architects as Whidden and Lewis, A.E. Doyle and Pietro Belluschi would satisfy the clamoring of the city's inhabitants for larger, more innovative buildings and a more cosmopolitan architecture.

3103 - Portland Rose.

By the mid-1920s, all the prestigious European revival styles—from Italianate to Georgian to French Second Empire—were represented in the urban landscape. Firms led by Doyle, Reid and Reid, and Sutton and Whitney had colonized the city's increasing muscular core with banks, department stores, office buildings and warehouses. With sky-loggias and Ionic colonnades advertising the imperial myths of ancient Rome, buildings such as Jackson Tower, U.S. National Bank, the Benson Hotel and Meier & Frank stood guard over the urban theater, proclaiming the city's architectural ambitions. By the end of the decade, the city's downtown was one massive terra cotta pavilion, in which the design genius of Portland's premier architects had shiningly materialized.

Elsewhere in the city, a network of verdant oases also had been cultivated. An extensive park system including Laurelhurst, Peninsula and Washington parks had blossomed with roses and rhododenron. These additions introduced the public to a new architectural order that sought to mirror idealized European scenes characterized by palatial buildings, bridges, plush hotels, elegant restaurants, tea gardens, expansive parks and open plazas.

During the 1930s, the urban landscape would move in an entirely new direction. On the streets west of Portland's terra cotta stronghold, scintillating zigzags and applied polychrome ornamentation would grace fashionable apartment houses and medical office buildings. And in 1948, Belluschi's design for the Equitable Building would herald the coming of a new, modernistic age. A triumph in technologic expressionism, the Equitable was the first building in the country to be completely sealed, the first to use double-glazed windows and the first to be sheathed in aluminum.

In the past three decades, Portland has established a powerful and radically different scale to its downtown skyline. A constant source of visual excitement, the city today is dotted with rare architectural specimens, among them: a whimsical public square filled with copious historical allusions, a pink skyscraper that performs luminous metamorphoses against the region's cloud-mottled skies, and a painted polychrome building that looks like a cross between a Belgian truffle and Wurlitzer jukebox. The result of all this hubris is a scintillating collage where—on trim 200-foot-long blocks—the styled architecture of a noble past is knuckled against sleek, aluminum-clad towers that point toward the "World of Tomorrow."

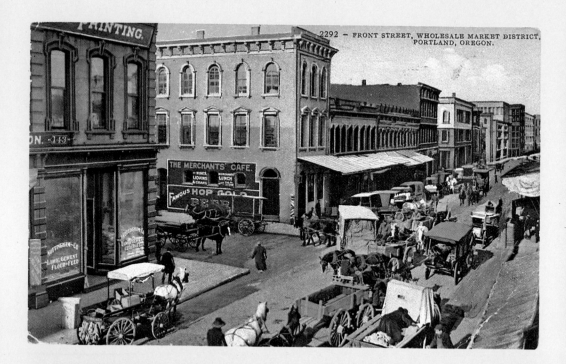

2292 – FRONT STREET, WHOLESALE MARKET DISTRICT, PORTLAND, OREGON.

Third Street, Portland, Oregon.

OREGON, Sixth Street, Portland.

Fourth Street, Portland, Oregon.

With its broad boulevards, exquisite parks and Beaux Arts-style buildings, Portland developed along European sensibilities. One architecture critic waxed poetic about a city "strong in natural beauty and turn-of-the-century civilization in the form of fine classical buildings that…add splendor to the Athens of the West."

Morrison Street, Portland, Oregon.

Morrison Street, East from 6th St., Portland, Oregon.

374. BUSINESS SECTION FROM THE HARBOR, PORTLAND, OREGON.

703 BUSINESS DISTRICT FROM BROADWAY AND SALMON STREETS, PORTLAND, OREGON

716 BROADWAY NORTH FROM MAIN AT NIGHT, PORTLAND, OREGON

The messy vitality of Portland's popular culture has been broadcast by neon lights and other forms of illumination since the early part of the century. Lighted arches extended along Third Avenue in 1905, serving as a canopy for festive events. Since the early part of the century, the Portland Design Commission has encouraged the development of a unique sign district to create an exuberant atmosphere along its commercial corridors.

103. THIRD STREET, PORTLAND, ORE., AT NIGHT.

146. EMPRESS THEATRE, PORTLAND, ORE.

Lipman Wolfe, New Department Store. Portland, Oregon.

122. UNION DEPOT, PORTLAND, ORE.

Montgomery Ward & Co., Portland, Ore.

New Multnomah County Court House, Portland, Ore.

1405. The Public Library, Portland, Oregon.

City Hall, Portland, Ore.

NEW FEDERAL POST OFFICE, PORTLAND, OREGON

Portland Central Bus Depot, Portland, Oregon   29

New Home of The Oregonian, Portland's Largest Newspaper.

Mt. Hood, from Portland, Oregon

Portland Stock Yards, Portland, Ore.

PORTLAND PLANT
OCCUPIES 1000 FEET OF
RIVER FRONT
12 ACRES FLOOR SPACE

Skidmore Fountain, PORTLAND, Oregon.

"Meet you at the fountain," was a popular expression during the 1890s, when Skidmore Fountain was the center of Portland night life. A gift of Stephen Skidmore and sculpted by Olin M. Warner, the fountain consists of a granite base carved into a horse trough, supplied with water pouring forth from lions' heads. It bears the inscription: "Good citizens are the riches of a city."

928 - OREGONIAN BUILDING, PORTLAND, OREGON.

5043 Hotel Oregon, Portland, Ore.

Journal Building,
Portland, Oregon.

Portland High School, Portland, Ore.

Temple Beth Israel,
Portland, Ore.

PUBLIC SERVICE BUILDING, PORTLAND, OREGON   53

New Equitable Building, Portland, Oregon.

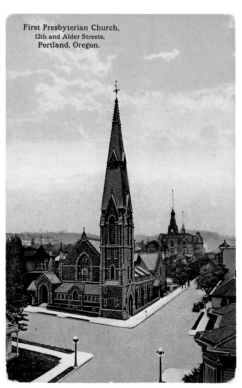

First Presbyterian Church,
12th and Alder Streets,
Portland, Oregon.

Picture postcards have long celebrated the fact that Portland is a "city of bridges." St. Johns Bridge, one of America's most beautiful suspension spans, was designed and built by Robinson and Steinman, a New York City bridge engineering firm.

1795- Elk Fountain, Plaza Park, Portland, Oregon.

In 1925, as a young man of 25, my mind already partially molded by the traditions of a classical culture, I had the good fortune to arrive in Portland, where I was exposed to a place still wild and unburdened by the past, a place bursting with the energy of youth. What I found was a city uniquely shaped by nature, climate and the pride and toil of determined pioneers. Here, I thought, was the future. And Portland seemed a lively symbol of all that was yet to come.

Today, at the end of a long life, I find no greater meaning than to have shared in the growth and flowering of such a beautiful place.

—Pietro Belluschi

PARKS AND PLACES

From the heights of Washington Park to the lowlands of Laurelhurst Park, Portland presents a vista of verdant hillsides, manicured gardens, and homes draped with foliage. The seeds for its park system were planted in 1903 when John C. Olmsted arrived in the city for the dual mission of planning the Lewis and Clark Exposition and discussing a park program for the city. Washington Park is known for its world-class rose garden and adjoining Japanese Gardens, Laurelhurst Park for its profuse shrubbery and artificial lake stocked with ducks and swans, and the Sanctuary of Our Sorrowful Mother for its Italian wood-carvings, open air grotto and 21 sanctuaries.

OREGON, The Plaza, Portland.

Vista Ave., leading to Portland Heights, showing beautiful houses and rose hedges, Portland, Ore.

OREGON, A Portland Home.

205 A Beautiful View in Laurelhurst Park, Portland, Oregon.

293. CITY PARK, PORTLAND, OREGON.

10:—Fountain and Band Stand in Peninsula Rose Gardens, Portland, Ore.

12:—View in Laurelhurst Park, Portland, Oregon.

742—SPRING TIME, LAMBERT GARDENS, PORTLAND, OREGON

727 COURT OF ROSE FESTIVAL QUEEN, LAMBERT GARDENS, PORTLAND, OREGON

The Monastery, Sanctuary of Our Sorrowful Mother, Portland, Oregon

Scene in Laurelhurst Park, Portland, Oregon

LAURELHURST PARK, PORTLAND, OREGON

Picking Roses,
Portland, Oregon.

City Park, Portland, Oregon.

Portland and King's Height. The most Beautiful Residence
District on Earth. Portland, Ore.

Council Crest, the Dreamland of the Northwest, Portland, Oregon.

177:—New Jantzen Beach, Portland, Ore.

"The Oaks" An Amusement Resort, Portland, Oregon.

Shooting the Chutes at the Oaks, Portland, Ore.

Postcards from Oaks Amusement Park, Jantzen Beach, and Council Crest Park give a glimpse of Portland's unique ability to combine scenic beauty with healthy recreational pursuits. During its heyday in the 1930s and 1940s, Jantzen Beach would host 4,000 dancers nightly in its Golden Canopy Ballroom. To get in shape for those nights of "dancin' at Jantzen," foxtrotters spent their daytime hours pursuing the secret of health and beauty at one of the park's four swimming pools.

Polar Bear in City Park, Portland, Oregon.

MOUNT HOOD FROM PORTLAND, ORE.

136. HOTEL PORTLAND, PORTLAND, ORE.

"MAIN PARLOR, HOTEL PORTLAND, PORTLAND, ORE."

THE PORTLAND HOTEL

The Portland Hotel, which stood on the site of the present Pioneer Courthouse Square, was the symbolic hub of the city between 1890 and 1949. "This famous hostelry for years has been this city's guest house, occupying an entire block in the middle of the city, yet it has an atmosphere of seclusion," ran the description published in the 1948-49 edition of Capitol's Who's Who For Oregon. "Notable is the hotel's open courtyard and its grassy plot and fragrant blooms and vine-clad veranda. Every room is an outside room...and from its upper windows may be seen the green heights above the city, the Cascades, the snow-clad peaks and the famous Mt. Hood."

Court of Hotel Portland, Decorated For Rose Festival Portland, Oregon.

PORTLAND HOTEL COURT, PORTLAND, ORE.

Portland Hotel, Portland, Ore.

Portland Hotel, Portland, Oregon.

ROOM WITH A VIEW

THE MALLORY HOTEL — 15th AND YAMHILL, PORTLAND, OREGON

One of the city's quiet and understated hotels, the Mallory, to this day, features the same round bed in its "honeymoon suite."

Pretty girls, Pretty girls everywhere, But the PORTLAND BELLES are claimed most fair.

Multnomah Hotel, Portland, Ore.

The Round Bed at the Mallory Hotel

S. W. MORRISON, FROM 12th TO 13th STREETS — PORTLAND, ORE.

FREE GARAGE
HOTEL
DANMOORE

DANMOORE HOTEL

Coffee Shop

Section of the Lobby

HOTEL MULTNOMAH — PORTLAND, OREGON

6A-H994

HOTEL SEWARD—
HOUSE OF CHEER
10th and Alder Streets
W. C. CULBERTSON,
Proprietor,
Portland, Oregon.

HEATHMAN HOTELS

HEATHMAN HOTEL

NEW HEATHMAN HOTEL

Shangri-La — MOTEL

PORTLAND'S NEWEST AND FINEST MOTEL
6828 NORTHEAST UNION AVENUE
PORTLAND 11, OREGON

Breeze Hill MOTEL AAA

11240 S. W. PACIFIC HIGHWAY
PORTLAND 19, OREGON

One of Portland's Finest Motels

Bruer's Tower Restaurant

9656 S. W. Barbur Blvd. (U. S. 99W)
PORTLAND, OREGON

AT SEATTLE, WASH.

AT SALT LAKE CITY, UTAH

Nationally Famous — COON CHICKEN INN — 5474 Sandy Blvd. — PORTLAND, OREGON

With marble-clad walls, fluted columns and mosaic tile floors, Portland's upscale eating establishments of the 1920s captured a distinctly Parisian air.

ROOF GARDEN, THE BOWERS
11th and Stark Streets, Portland, Ore.

YE MAGIC LANTERN INN, ACROSS FROM MAJESTIC THEATRE, ON PARK ST. (UPSTAIRS), PORTLAND, OREGON.

PAGO-PAGO - 525 S. W. STARK - PORTLAND, ORE.
AMERICA'S MOST BEAUTIFUL TROPICAL ROOM

"Soda Fountain." The Hazelwood Cream Store,
388—90 Washington St., Portland, Ore.

BOTH PHONES
MAIN 919
A 1191

THE QUELLE CAFE

HOME OF THE CRAWFISH

FIRST CLASS
RESTAURANT
SERVICE

6TH & STARK STS.
PORTLAND · OREGON

"THE PLACE THAT MADE CRAWFISH FAMOUS"

FRED SECHTEM & J. E. FALT, PROPS.

Tea Room on Roof Garden, Nortonia Hotel,
11th and Washington Sts., Portland, Ore.

Interior of Swetland's,
Portland Oreg.

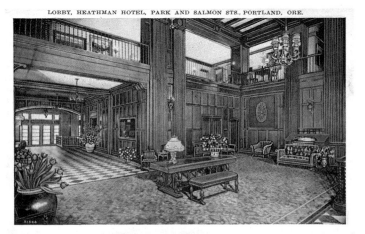

LOBBY, HEATHMAN HOTEL, PARK AND SALMON STS., PORTLAND, ORE.

Swetland's Soda Fountain,
Portland Ore.

AT THE BEACH

The evening train from Seaside to Portland runs no longer. As for Bay Ocean City, it was swallowed by the sea more than half-a-century ago. What is left, though, is a long, lonesome road. A road where you can stop your car at a bend high above a crescent-shaped beach dotted with craggy monoliths and strain to hear the ragged roar of sea lions through the dull rumble of waves far below. From Astoria to Brookings, U.S. Highway 101 slithers 397 miles along the serpentine coastline, sometimes struggling along precipitous cliffs, as it does near Neahkahnie Mountain, where it climbs nearly 600 feet above the sea. It is an unpredictable road, playing hide and seek with basaltic cliffs, sand dunes, murmuring rivulets and spruce forests. In Florence and Pacific City, the blacktop dips into a vast expanse of sandy beach; near Tillamook Head, the road darts behind a rugged promontory where one can glimpse a primeval forest with its lush growth of rhododendron, salal, huckleberry and foxglove.

The Oregon coast flashes as many faces as a masked ball. In fact, so eclectic is its topography and climate, that individual sections could be grafted onto the wildly

Cannon Beach, Oregon Coast.

Copyright 1909, Adler Photo Co.

varied coastlines of 20 different countries across the world. In early spring as the fog rolls in from the sea, you may find yourself driving south from Cannon Beach through Arch Cape, Rockaway and Netarts, groping your way from one tiny hamlet to another. At least once each winter, in almost every coastal outpost, ominous thunderheads coalesce in the sky. Surreptitiously, as if they had a will of their own, clouds nestle against the Coastal Range and drop mega-buckets, splaying open a few rock slides here and there. But in the bloom of summer, the coastal complexion changes dramatically. The blazing sun clarifies the atmosphere and beaches from Seaside to Cape Blanco are kissed by briny offshore breezes that seem to have been propelled to land by giant, silk-bladed fans at the horizon's edge.

Raw, uncluttered and boasting fracture lines that attest to eons of geological torture, the Oregon coast is teeming with sea life. Easily observed from Boiler Bay Wayside, just south of Gleneden Beach, whales ply up and down the coast during their annual migrations while at Three Arch Rocks near Oceanside, sea lions have taken up permanent residence. The Oregon coast is sprinkled with state parks–Neptune, Honeyman and Oswald West to name just a few—and with everything from dramatic lighthouses and soaring bridges to tide pools and scenic picnic spots that offer unobstructed ocean-gazing. Just south of Cape Foulweather is Devil's Punchbowl, a cavernous gouge extending almost 100 feet into hard sandstone. Dubbed "The Devil's Washing Machine" by local residents, this chamber is nothing less than a giant hydraulic battering ram that offers its visitors a behind-the-scenes look at how shorelines are formed.

Whether hunting for gemstone treasures or glass floats at Agate Beach, digging for clams near Rockaway, or casting for shad or salmon near Coos Bay, one cannot help but be intrigued by the face-off between land and water on the Oregon coast. Here, two titanic forces—one stationary and one in motion—engage in eternal dispute. Giant outcroppings of rock spotwelded to offshore sites near Cannon Beach, Arch Cape and Bandon are stark testimonials to this ceaseless dialogue between nature's elemental forces.

An entirely different, almost alien landscape stretches for more than 40 miles between Coos Bay and Florence on the state's southern shore. Undulating from the ocean inland for up to three miles, the Oregon Dunes National Recreation Area

Moore Hotel and Tillamook Head, Seaside, Ore.

offers some of the most dramatic juxtapositions of sand, shadow and sky in the country. This is especially so in the early evening when the red-tinged rays just before sunset highlight stark shadows sandwiched between the thick, fleecy sky and rippling dunes.

As destiny would have it, the Oregon coast is also known for its passionate sunsets. From an Olympic vantage on Cape Lookout, Neahkahnie Mountain or Heceta Head, one can watch the sun making its final plunge beneath the Pacific horizon, leaving behind giant tufts of cotton candy clouds, whose edges glow a brilliant cerise. As the technicolor sky unfolds, the shoreline and cliffs swell with the polyrhythmic drone of water pummeling hourglass-fine sands and crickets jigging away at their perpetual rumba. Seagulls, wings outstretched in perfect arcs, search for thermals to take them away from the ocean's edge. Before long, the sky's dark canopy is frosted with stars and strips of blue-green luminescence appear and disappear at the crest of the tumbling nocturnal surf. By the time you're ready to turn in, the coastal glow has made everything in sight look like paradise, a place that never seems far away on the Oregon coast.

Salmon Cannery,
The largest plant on the Pacific Coast,
Astoria, Oregon.

Astoria, Oregon.

Tokeland Oyster Beds, near mouth of Columbia River.
Home of the famous "Toke Points."

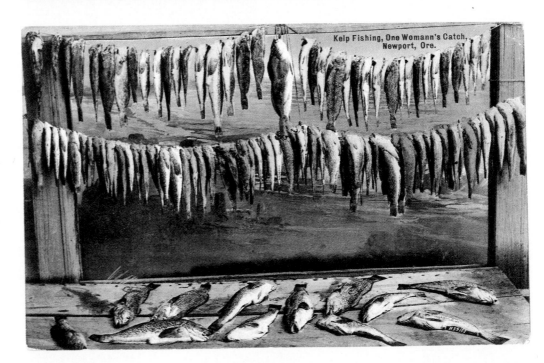

Kelp Fishing, One Womann's Catch,
Newport, Ore.

Facing Page: The Astoria fishing industry runs long and deep. At the turn of the century, salmon canneries crowded the waterfront. Albacore tuna and long-line shark fishing were popular in the 1930s and 1940s. More recently, the industry diversified and began to handle sole, rockfish, flounder and other varieties of white-meat fish that could be scooped from along the continental shelf.

Beached near Stevens State Park, The Peter Iredale was a British Vessel lost in 1906. Not much of the rusty hull remains, but what is left can be approached at times during low tide.

WRECK OF SHIP "PETER IREDALE" CLATSOP BEACH, ORE.

Water Front, Marshfield, Coos Co. Oregon.

S. S. "Rose City" leaving Astoria, Oregon for California Ports.

HOTEL SEASIDE,
SEASIDE, (The Trails End City) OREGON.

Necanicum River, Seaside, Oregon.

490 NATIVE GULLS, SEASIDE PROMENADE AND TILLAMOOK HEAD. OREGON COAST HIGHWAY

PHOTO BY MONTAG

2A155

485 HIGH TIDES, VIEW FROM PROMENADE, SEASIDE, OREGON

PHOTO BY MONTAG

OREGON COAST HIGHWAY AT THE END OF THE OLD OREGON TRAIL

Seaside was once the "Coney Island" of Oregon's oceanside communities. Its carnival atmosphere, superabundance of tourist facilities and long stretch of beach thrive to this day.

The Shell Road, Seaside, Oregon.

1005   CAPE ARAGO BRIDGE AND LIGHTHOUSE MOUTH OF COOS BAY, OREGON COAST HIGHWAY

PHOTO BY WESLEY ANDREWS

9A-H891

985   COOS BAY BRIDGE, NORTH BEND, OREGON

PHOTO BY WESLEY ANDREWS

OREGON COAST HIGHWAY

983   SIUSLAW RIVER BRIDGE, FLORENCE, OREGON

PHOTO BY WESLEY ANDREWS

OREGON COAST HIGHWAY

981   YAQUINA BAY BRIDGE, NEWPORT, OREGON

PHOTO BY WESLEY ANDREWS

OREGON COAST HIGHWAY

One of Oregon's most celebrated photographers, Wesley Andrews, took the original black-and-white photos that were used to make linen postcards of the state's magnificent network of coastal bridges. The Yaquina Bay Bridge is a graceful cantilever structure completed in 1936. Rising to 138 feet above the channel, the bridge deck is high enough to permit passage of ocean-going vessels. Nearly a mile in length, the Coos Bay Bridge comprises a series of concrete arches that flank three suspension-type bridges that carry US 101 more than 150 feet above a busy channel.

948 UMPQUA LIGHT HOUSE, OREGON COAST HIGHWAY

PHOTO BY WESLEY ANDREWS

7A-H3958

989 YAQUINA LIGHT HOUSE, YAQUINA HEAD

PHOTO BY WESLEY ANDREWS

OREGON COAST HIGHWAY

Tillamook Lighthouse, near Seaside, Ore.

Arago Light House Coos Bay, Oregon.

Marshfield High School Coos Co. Oregon.

967 DEVIL'S PUNCH BOWL AND GULL ISLAND, OREGON COAST HIGHWAY

PHOTO BY HOME STUDIO, TOLEDO   2A181

ARCH IN JUMP OFF JOE, NEWPORT, ORE.

Road around Hug Point,
Canon Beach near Seaside, Ore.

The origins of the name Jump Off Joe long have been lost in myths of jilted lovers, fleeing outlaws and drunken brawls. But this fellow, contentedly sucking on his pipe, seems bent on a more contemplative pursuit.

"Tillamook, Oregon"

MAIN PLANT OF WORLD-FAMOUS TILLAMOOK CHEESE
ON HIGHWAY 101 NEAR TILLAMOOK, OREGON

Milking Jersey Cows on an Oregon Dairy Farm.

Living on the edge of the land, with the broad sweep of the Pacific stretching across the horizon outside the window, and having a personal cycle that finds the middle of the night most conducive to productive work, provides opportunities to see the world from an unusual perspective.

Moonsets are fascinating, especially in the deep of the night with a bright, full moon. The pocked face glows as though lit from within, and its luminance glistens off the water with an undulating silvery brightness. The moon's white light dispels the deep black, but with the eerie feeling of noon painted with midnight's brush.

There is no color then, only stark contrasts and deep shadows muting details. Shimmering, dimpling brightness rides easily on invisible liquid swells, then erupts into high-rolling breakers racing for the shore. White sudsy foam scrubs shiny black rocks on the beach. Leaves and stems nearest the light of the tall ancient firs and windblown salal are faintly outlined by reflecting moisture, only to fade in the flat shadows into deep black silhouette stirring in the wind. It is a surrealisitic scene in living black and white.

—JEAN M. AUEL

990. Moonlight on Tillamook Bay, Oregon.
ON THE P. R. & N. RAILROAD.

U.S. HIGHWAY 101 . . . Coquille's Newest . . . COQUILLE, OREGON

Devil's Causeway, Newport, Ore.

Seaside, Oregon,
Departure of the evening train for Portland.

Playing on the Beach, Seaside, Oregon.

"I am gaining in strength daily"
on the Coast of Oregon.
near Seaside

Digging Rock Oysters,
Newport, Oregon.

Harbor View, Bandon, Oregon

Hunting Agates at Jump off Joe, Newport, Ore.

962 THE SEAWARD DUNES OF PACIFIC SHORES, OREGON COAST HIGHWAY

2A177

969 BANDON BEACH, OREGON COAST HIGHWAY

PHOTO BY CROXALL STUDIO

2A183

Scene on Cannon Beach, Oregon.

FIELD AND STREAM

Oregon remains the sort of place where a man, given the necessities—a blade, a pole, a length of twine—can head into the woods and live off the land. The spirit of the buckskin-clad mountain men, who did exactly that, still echoes in the myriad ways Oregonians bask in the bounty of their territory. Nothing better reveals this passion than the scene played out each winter on the banks of countless coastal streams. It is then that waters run cold. Cold enough for steelhead. Faces etched in determination, fingers numb with forgotten pain, fishermen wait, hip deep in hope. Hour after hour, they pursue the mightiest—and the most elusive—of all fighting fish. Many go months without so much as a single bite. Some wait years to land one. Some never do. But time after time they return, immutably locked to the challenge of wresting a prize from Mother Nature's hand.

Steelhead may be elusive, but sturgeon are just plain hard to handle. In the 1930s, a Hell's Canyon prospector recalled the method old-timers used for hauling sturgeon from the Snake. "These goldurned ranchers here on both sides of the river, they just take a good stout line, almost as big as a rope with a helluva big hook and

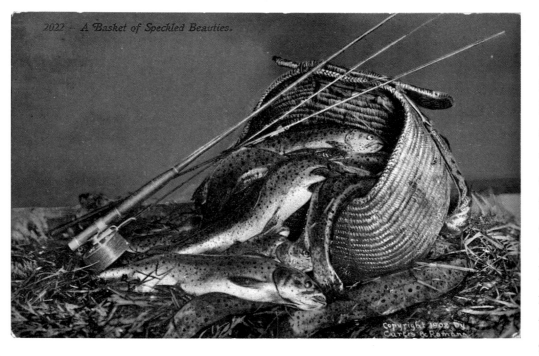

2022 – A Basket of Speckled Beauties.

put a hunk of meat on it and let 'er trail slow-like, and when they get a bite they haul in on her and start up the bank with the line tied to the horn o' the saddle and if the horse is strong enough they yank the brute outer the water—and say, I'm tellin' yer they is monsters. Them fish must be some kind of fish what didn't git inter the Ark."

Big fish, even escapees from the Ark, are not the sole quarry of Oregon's outdoorsmen. Hunters by the thousand roam the hills each fall. For many, the annual armed sortie is as much a matter of communion with wild places as it is a pursuit of deer, elk and bear. Or at least that often is the tale told by those who return empty-handed. Whatever the motivation, one thing seems certain: A hunting trip remains a reaffirmation of man's place in the universe, an opportunity to simultaneously stalk like a giant on the evolutionary stage, and yet be dwarfed by the power of nature in the raw.

Others pursue a more gentle path into the wilderness—taking only memories, leaving only footprints. Armed with nothing more than a backpack, a bag of trail mix, and a layer of Gore-Tex, they happily haul themselves off the beaten track. Roaming the trails of Three Sisters and Eagle Cap, running the rapids of the Rogue and the Deschutes, skiing the slopes of Hood and Bachelor, or simply picnicking beside some sylvan stream, they find space enough and solace to recharge the batteries of the human condition.

Oregon may seem to resonate with a panoply of produce, but earliest efforts to cultivate its bounty were less than auspicious. In 1810, Nathan Winship, Oregon's first farmer, sailed with a cargo of hogs and goats into the Columbia and promptly set about planting seeds along the river's banks. Winship's venture was doomed to failure: The Columbia rose quicker than his crops. By 1825, however, Dr. John McLoughlin, chief factor of the Hudson's Bay Company, was successfully farming at Fort Vancouver. Three years later, veteran trapper Etienne Lucier, retiring to more sedentary pursuits, planted wheat on the east bank of the Willamette River, near the present site of Portland. By 1846, more than 160,000 bushels of wheat were being raised in the state. Favorable reports of fertile valleys and the cry of "Free land!" soon began filtering east. Pioneers loaded up covered wagons and hit the Oregon Trail.

Today, along the Willamette River in the flush of summer, where the land is so

2308 – MT. HOOD OREGON AND THE MONARCH OF THE MOUNTAIN.

fertile even fenceposts threaten to put down roots and burst into bloom, crops crowd so close that every nook and cranny seem to hum with the energy of growth. Here, where settlers first gazed in awe upon the promise that had drawn them clear across the continent, the soil yields grain, fruit, vegetables—and the seeds that turn the lawns of America Oregon-green.

When spring breaks over the Hood River Valley, there is nothing coy about the cornucopia about to be unleashed. The afternoon air seems heavy with the fragrance of fertility as acre after tree-studded acre boughs bow beneath the weight of blossom. And as light fades, and evening's gentle breezes come to play tag among the orchards, the land seems to tease with the promise of fruitful days in store.

Even in the backyard of the average Portland gardener, with the least amount of effort, a raised bed or two will produce buckets of tomatoes, entire volumes of lettuce, and so much zucchini that a man can lose friends just trying to give the stuff away. Lucier's wheat field may long since have been swallowed up by the hungry metropolis, but the legacy of the seeds he planted colors today the furthermost reaches of the state he once roamed.

Beautiful Oregon.
The Head Waters of Rogue River.

HOME OF THE BIG RAINBOW TROUT,
DESCHUTES RIVER IN SCENIC OREGON—P160

"Result of an Afternoon's Wild Goose Hunt" in Oregon.

FUR TRADERS' CAMP, OREGON.

FISHING IN THE STREAM   S-460

GREETINGS FROM BEND, OREGON   4A-H2162

255. "THIS IS THE LIFE." ENJOYING AN OUTING ON THE SHORES OF THE WILLAMETTE RIVER, OREGON.

S-447

GREETINGS FROM ALBANY, OREGON, NEAR CAMP ADAIR   NO. 669

TROUT FISHING IN THE BEAUTIFUL STREAMS OF THE CASCADE MOUNTAINS, OREGON

Spraying Fruit Trees in Oregon.

Willamette Valley Hop Field.

Picking Strawberries in Oregon.

Digging Potatoes in Oregon.

TIMBER

Oregon's earliest settlers didn't exactly conduct a love affair with timber. No sooner had a pioneer set down his axe from clearing a piece of land than trees seemed to start growing over. Men found themselves engaged in a battle with a landscape so fecund it seemed to fight back. East of the Cascades, trees may have been well enough behaved. Legions of lodgepole and Ponderosa pine marched in relative order. But west of the mountains was a different story. Up and down the roller coaster of rain-blessed slopes, Douglas fir, spruce and cedar ran amok in an anarchy of unbridled growth.

At first, only shipwrights highly prized these mammoth virgin forests. In 1792, George Vancouver was delighted by the gloriously straight conifer he found to replace the mast on his ship, the Discovery. By the 1820s, however, Dr. John McLoughlin had built the Northwest's first water-powered sawmill near Fort Vancouver to supply boards for Oregon's first frame houses. Within a few years, he was shipping lumber to San Francisco, to the Hawaiian islands, even to China. For Oregon, the era of green gold had dawned.

The first steam-driven mill, with its tireless circular saw, began operating in Portland in 1850. From the start, the timber industry was one of innovation and ingenuity. It quickly became apparent that horse logging,

No. 510. Lumbering, Oregon.

which had swept like a scythe through entire forests as fallers relentlessly harvested their way west, would bog down in Oregon mud. So loggers turned to oxen. To make their task easier, bullwhackers pushing into the hills around Portland first cleared paths through the forest then fashioned crude roads by felling smaller trees crosswise across these trails. As grease monkeys spread dogfish oil to reduce friction on these "skid roads," man and beast set to hauling the great logs toward the mills.

As the industry matured and the demand for ever-bigger logs increased, timberman John Dolbeer became frustrated with oxen. He built a crude donkey engine with a single cylinder and an upright boiler. At first, loggers laughed at this strange contraption. But there would be no turning back. Mechanization had come to the woods. Within a few years, the roar of machinery had drowned the whistling of ox drivers just as the scream of the chainsaw would one day end the singing of the "misery whip" hand-held saw.

Skid roads were not the only tricks loggers employed to move their mammoth trees. Some lumber operations installed flumes, elevated wooden canals down which logs plummeted at breakneck speeds. There are many tales of thirsty loggers who, eager to escape the woods, risked riding logs down flumes in perilous shortcuts to a Saturday night on the town.

And always, the bigger trees beckoned from higher up the slopes. In the 1870s, Ephraim Shay built his first geared locomotive, and railroads began to inch their way into stands of timber so steep old-timers had sworn they would never be reached by rail. In the relentless drive to cross the steep-sided valleys and to harvest the finest lumber, loggers began throwing up great trestles that created the most formidable architecture of the woods.

Although it provided the backbone of Oregon's ascent to economic and cultural maturity, the timber trade took a fearful toll in backs, bones and bodies. After months of work in a lumber camp, loggers were ready to cut loose. And Portland, the supposedly sedate New England lady of the Northwest, was ready to accommodate. At Gus Erickson's saloon, 50 bartenders poured sustenance across the longest bar in the world. Apparently drink was not the sole recreation. At the three-story Paris House, the long arm of the law once detained 83 "strumpets" in a single raid. Both bar and bawdy house may be gone, but one legacy of those times—lumberman Simon Benson's 20 bronze drinking fountains, an attempt to slake the thirst of his workers with Bull Run brew—survives.

If the rewards of the forest industry were enormous, begetting the great lumber fortunes that provided the basis for Portland prosperity in the twentieth century,

In the Oregon Woods.

the costs, too, were high. And not just in terms of life and limb. The land paid its price. In the 1930s, the area west of Portland to the ocean still was one vast, virgin forest. Trees up to 30-feet in circumference towered 300-feet toward the sky. On the morning of August 14, 1933, a few miles out of Glenwood, a small fire broke out at a logging operation, and a second fire, its origins undetermined, erupted in the nearby woods. The Tillamook Burn consumed millions of trees, thousands of animals, and devastated 311,000 acres.

Subsequent efforts to restore the forest, a process that continued through decades, helped engender in citizens the passion for conservation that has become such an integral element of the Oregon ethos in the second half of the twentieth century. In the protected watersheds, horse logging, with steeds wearing diapers, helps to preserve the delicate ecological balance so critical to riparian areas. Meanwhile, overhead, helicopters and balloons ferry logs from ridges off limits to logging trucks. The timber industry, no longer encouraged to pursue hellbent exploitation of a natural resource, finds itself instead charged with nurturing a renewable resource, with serving as guardian of a sacred trust. Oregonians approach the 21st century insisting that one opportunity remain inviolate: the chance to roam deep into dark forests and seek there transcendence among tall trees.

Hauling Logs to Mill in Oregon.

TAKING DONKEY UP MOUNTAIN SIDE.

Floating Logs, Oregon City, Oregon.

A Single " Oregon Fir, " cut in sections for transportation

Two Natives of Oregon,
A Bear Den and Dwelling in a Oregon Saw Log.
"In the Northwest."

NORTHERN PACIFIC 69318

Cedar Stump Residence, Oregon

From the earliest days, Oregonians have crafted homes from the giants of the forest. But few have matched the ingenuity of the folk portrayed in these postcards. The bear and his keeper maintained a respectable distance—living at opposite ends of this rolling roadside attraction. The family—ma, pa and the three kids—carved humble quarters from this cedar stump.

Oregon discovered
     soars natures' bounty
               to
snow-dipped summits
          while West the ocean
not too gently tests the coastal rock—
mighty limit to land
                    and

                         sea.
Flowers in February
          bloom an avalanche of color
through months elsewhere
          somber
Oregon,
          beauty-strewn with the complex gifts
of Divine delight—
Oregon endowed,
          majestic, comforting, rugged
                hospitable
                         casual and causal—
Extraordinary Oregon
     Contemplates its people
and daily beckons us
to humanly repay
          with remnants of our betterselves
               the
                    given
                         splendor

                              —JAMES DEPREIST

Southern Pacific Passenger Train in
Cow Creek Canon, Oregon.

Lumber Scene.

5986. Trestle thru Timberbelt, Oregon.
ON THE P. R. & N. RAILROAD.

HAULING PINE LOGS IN THE SCENIC PACIFIC NORTHWEST P103

DOWN IN THE VALLEY

The heart of Oregon, as the Willamette Valley is sometimes called, is anchored by a snaking river that runs 186 miles through rolling farms and timber lands from the Calapooya Mountains to the Columbia River. "The Willamette River is a stream which the ancient poets would have peopled with nymphs and celebrated in song," wrote Salem Judge J. Quinn Thornton more than a century ago. "Its waters are transparent and upon its bosom ducks, cranes, swans, pelicans and other water-fowl with variegated vestments glide gracefully or patter their broad bills among the reeds and grasses of the shore." Those who live, work and play in this enchanted valley, where fruit and nut orchards threaten to collapse beneath the weight of their own bounty, will testify that Thornton's sentiments have stood the test of time. Home of two-thirds of the state's population, the Willamette Valley is a land of seemingly inexhaustible fertility, swelling into crop-riddled rises and then sinking again into seed-strewn hollows that stretch away in picturesque beauty.

Draining a verdant expanse of land overlooked by forested heights and rimmed with flower-strewn fields, the Willamette connects some of the state's most active

Boating on the Mill Race, EUGENE, Oregon.

commercial and educational centers including Portland, Salem, Corvallis and Eugene. Much of the region's early history can be traced to Methodist clergyman Jason Lee and his nephew, Daniel Lee, who mounted their horses and followed the "Oregon Trail." Leaving the Atlantic Coast in March, 1834, they arrived in Oregon in September of the same year. In 1835, they established a Methodist mission station—its stated purpose was to Christianize the Indians—and a school on a plot where would one day rise downtown Salem. Consisting at that time of a quaint one-story log cottage, the school was taken over by Oregon Insititute in 1842, making Willamette University the oldest institution of higher learning in the Pacific Northwest.

Although towns such as Oregon City, Cottage Grove and Corvallis are known for their tranquil streets with sidewalks shaded by acacias and maple trees, the valley also boasts a rich architectural heritage. One of the region's most celebrated buildings is the present State Capitol, which replaced the original structure destroyed by fire in 1935. Designed by New York architect Francis Kelly—in association with the Oregon firm of Whitehouse and Church—the Capitol features an exterior cylindrical dome that resembles a fluted column and a majestic interior finished in Travertine Rose, a marble-like stone from Montana. Four large murals depicting milestones in the State's history decorate the rotunda's upper walls. The two works by Barry Faulkner recreate Captain Gray's landing at the mouth of the Columbia and Dr. John McLoughlin's welcoming of settlers at Fort Vancouver. Murals by New York artist Frank Swartz depict the Lewis and Clark expedition at Celilo Falls and a wagon train in the mid-1800s.

Eugene is the cultural and industrial center of the upper Willamette Valley. In 1846, its founder, Eugene F. Skinner, built a crude log cabin at the foot of a small hillock known to the Calapooya Indians as Ya-po-ah, where his wife gave birth to the first white child born in Lane County. The University of Oregon was officially established in 1876, with much of its financing provided by private pledges from local residents. Farmers without cash donated wheat; one gave a fat hog. A scholarly tradition in architecture was formally launched in 1916 when Ellis Lawrence established the university's school of architecture. Lawrence had an uncanny ability for melding a variety of styles—from Egyptian to Art Deco—in his

State Capitol and Grounds, Salem, Oregon

designs for the Leaburg Power Station and for the part-Islam, part Romanesque Museum of Art on the university campus.

Home of Oregon State University, Corvallis sits on the west bank of the Willamette River just below its confluence with Marys River. Derived from the Latin phrase meaning, "heart of the valley," Corvallis was settled on land purchased from the Calapooya Indians. Soothed by its setting, contemporary life in this Willamette Valley outpost has not changed much from the 1860s when Theodor Kirchoff, a German merchant, traveler and author described it this way: "A friendly town in an idyllic setting...ramose trees along the streets, groves on the outskirts, and a view of the foothills of the Coast Range only three miles away... I recommend Corvallis to anyone seeking a quiet, rural environment and honest people innocent of 'Europe's veneer of politeness.'" One hundred years ago, it was the lure of the Willamette Valley, with its fabled fertility and cooperative climate, that drew the hardy hordes of settlers who made their way in covered wagons along the Oregon Trail. Viewed today from any of a thousand vantage points, the valley still resonates with that promise.

WILLAMETTE STREET, LOOKING NORTH FROM 11TH STREET, EUGENE, ORE.—8

Oregon State Capitol Building, Salem, Oregon

MEMORIAL UNION BUILDING, OREGON STATE COLLEGE, CORVALLIS, OREGON

THE MALL, UNIVERSITY OF OREGON CAMPUS, EUGENE, OREGON—2

Dickensian ghosts haunt these views of the State Reform School, but there is no record of any youngster here ever having disturbed the decorum of the dining room by daring to ask: "Please, Sir, may I have some more?"

It is misleading to think of the Willamette as just a valley. That would suggest a vague flatness buttressed by walls of earth. To consider the Willamette Valley, with its lush, rolling hills; fields of flowers and seed crops; tens of thousands of sheep; farms, subdivisions and modern townhouses, arranged around the meandering and tranquil Willamette River and its many branches and forks is to give form and substance to the diversity and richness that is Oregon. That is our Willamette Valley.

Much more than just a pretty face, however, the Willamette Valley is home to almost half of all Oregonians. Our children go to the many fine colleges in the valley. We thrive on the rich crops and welcome the temperate climate.

My own travels through Oregon frequently take me through the valley, as a destination in itself and as a gateway to the south, to the coast and to the Cascades. Oregon is a beautiful state, and the Willamette Valley a lovely and important region on its own. I guess I would call it our own Shangri-la.

—SEN. BOB PACKWOOD

A Farmer's Home in Oregon.

Town and Country

A pastoral air pervades early glimpses of urban settlement in Oregon. Salem seems nothing more than a collection of close-knit farmsteads. Newport hugs the shoreline, a sliver of enterprise squeezed between the ever-encroaching forest and the tireless echoing of the waves.

Salem, Oregon, as seen from Fairmount Park.

Main Street, Pendleton, Oregon

11th Street Eugene, Oregon

Beautiful Oregon — Klamath River, Klamath Falls

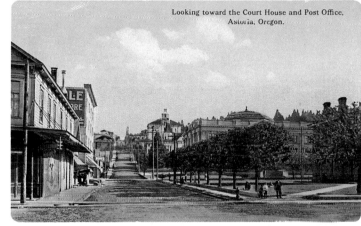

Looking toward the Court House and Post Office, Astoria, Oregon.

Wau Gwin Gwin Hotel, Hood River, Oregon

Broadway Street, Estacada, Oregon

Newport, Ore.

CELEBRATIONS

There is no record of the very first party thrown in Oregon. But one thing is certain. No sooner did settlers arrive, clear some land, throw up cabins and raise their crops than they invited over their neighbors, reached for their fiddles and kicked up a heel or two. Oregonians have been celebrating the bounty of their land ever since.

Today, in festivals all across the state, people come together to celebrate everything from seafood to Shakespeare, bronco bustin' to bird watching, garlic to grapes.

In 1885, Portland dry goods merchant Dan McAllen conceived the idea of a great fair to celebrate the centennial of the arrival of Meriwether Lewis and William Clark in Oregon. It was understood from the start that McAllen's project would be an unapologetic act of boosterism, a bold, brash way for Portland to catapult itself from the economic depression of the early 1890s. By 1903, the city fathers, the state of Oregon and the federal government had thrown their weight behind the plan. The official name of the fair, The Lewis and Clark Centennial and American Pacific Exposition and Oriental Fair, made clear its aim to firmly establish Portland's position as the preeminent city of the Pacific Rim.

Decorated Automobile in PORTLAND, Ore., Rose Festival Parade.

A site on a former swamp in Northwest Portland that was nestled between the river and the hills and framed by snow-capped mountains was designed to showcase Oregon. As architectural director for this momentous civic celebration, Portlander Ion Lewis was charged with defining the architectural tone and with designing no less than six of the "theme" structures. Planning for the exposition had begun in earnest in 1902, at which time Portland's population stood at 161,000. Since the orchestration of an international fair was a formidable undertaking, it was not surprising that Lewis and the fair's directors chose to commission America's most celebrated landscape architect, Frederick Law Olmsted, to design an overarching plan for the exposition.

The United States Government Building, designed in the office of James Knox Taylor, architect of the U.S. Treasury, set the stylistic tone for what may have been the largest collection of "wedding cake" architecture in history. More than 1,000-feet long, the building's grandiose main facade consisted of a massive colonnade in the Corinthian order separating two large towers mannered in the Spanish style. From June 1 through October 15, more than 2 million visitors toured the fair. Some 21 nations joined in the festivities. Japan spent $1 million on its exhibit, where people ogled fine silks and porcelains. At the Carnival of Venice concession, hundreds of ballet dancers from Europe and a chorus from the Metropolitan Opera Company performed on a 400-foot stage as serenading gondoliers plied their way across the canal that separated the front row from the footlights. The exposition also boasted Wild Professor Barnes's celebrated pair of diving elk, plunging 40 feet from a ramp, headlong into a tank of water. The beasts were no backwoods phenomenon. By 1905 they were veterans of performances in London, Paris and Berlin.

Hard on the heels of the success of the Lewis and Clark Exposition—the final official balance sheet showed a tidy little profit of $84,461—Portland Mayor Harry Lane endorsed E.W. Rowe's idea for a "rose festival." The notion may have been new, but the festival that was to emerge had roots running deep into the Oregon territory. In 1835, at her wedding to Jason Lee, Anna Marian Pittman received as a gift the first rose bush to reach Oregon by way of the Horn. Years later, after Lee's Salem mission had been destroyed

OFFICIAL MAILING CARD
LEWIS & CLARK CENTENNIAL 1905
PORTLAND, OREGON

CENTENNIAL PARK AND EXPERIMENTAL GARDENS.

PUBLISHED BY B.B. RICH, OFFICIAL STATIONEP

by fire, John Minto found the bush, nurtured it and began to distribute cuttings around the countryside. Bushes planted in Portland flourished especially well and the city found an emblem to call its own.

The Portland Rose Society was founded in 1887. Two years later, it held its first show in a tent. In 1904, a "fiesta" was held in conjunction with the rose show, and flower-bedecked horse-drawn surreys ran on city streets. In 1907, the Portland Rose Festival was born. One notable feature of that first great pageant was the "Electrical Parade," a line of 20 illuminated trolley floats that showed off Portland's claim to be the world's first city with a long-distance power transmission line.

Turn of the century celebrations were not the sole preserve of Webfoots. By 1900, competition among buckaroos had long been part of life on the ranches of Eastern Oregon. In 1910, Pendleton decided to invite the toughest steer wrestlers and bull riders in the region to a Round-Up. The cry went out: "Let 'er buck!" Each September 50,000 people crowd into town to help Pendleton shuck its image as a modern center of agricultural commerce and bask again in the glory of a wide open Wild West town.

OFFICIAL MAILING CARD
LEWIS & CLARK CENTENNIAL, 1905
PORTLAND, OREGON.

Forestry Building.

PUBLISHED BY B. B. RICH, OFFICIAL STATIONER.

THE LEWIS & CLARK CENTENNIAL
PORTLAND · OREGON · 1905.

DENVER LITHO. CO.

1905
Lewis and Clark Centennial
and
American Pacific Exposition
and Oriental Fair.

PORTLAND, OREGON.

Exposition opens June 1, 1905; closes
October 15, 1905. Meet me on the Trail.

Yours truly,

OFFICIAL MAILING CARD
LEWIS & CLARK CENTENNIAL, 1905
PORTLAND, OREGON.

United States Government Building.

PUBLISHED BY B. B. RICH, OFFICIAL STATIONER.

OFFICIAL MAILING CARD
LEWIS & CLARK CENTENNIAL, 1905
PORTLAND, OREGON.

MANUFACTURES LIBERAL ARTS AND VARIED INDUSTRIES

Manufacturers Liberal Arts and Varied Industrial Building.

PUBLISHED BY B. B. RICH, OFFICIAL STATIONER.

These official cards for the Lewis and Clark Exposition were published by B. B. Rich of Portland. They included a set of ten color views printed on a luminous silver background.

Designed by Albert E. Doyle for the Lewis and Clark Exposition, the Forestry Building was also known as "the Parthenon of Oregon" and the "world's largest log cabin." Moody and gargantuan in scale—one million board feet of lumber went into its construction—the building expressed an unholy alliance between materials of the region and classical Greek architecture.

THE PENDLETON ROUND-UP

The Pendleton Round-Up has been an annual event since 1910, attracting thousands of visitors each September. In Let 'er Buck, a book about the Round-Up published in 1921, Charles Wellington Furlong described a town filled with high-grade outfitting shops "overflowing with gala-colored shirts of sheening silk or velvet, studded on the collar... big-sombreroed Mexicans puffing on cigarillos and heavy-set papoose-bearing squaws and beautiful daughters."

Old Stage Coach Race, The Round Up, Pendleton, Or.

INDIAN GIRL AT UMATILLA INDIAN AGENCY—P119

Steer Roping Contest at "The Round Up," Pendleton, Ore.

Round-up Time, Pendleton, Oregon

FIFTH ANNUAL
ROSE FESTIVAL
PORTLAND OREGON
JUNE 5TH-10TH
1911

GRAND ANNUAL
ROSE FESTIVAL
PORTLAND OREGON
JUNE 7TH 12TH
1909

SOUVENIR PORTLAND
Rose FESTIVAL
COPYRIGHTED BY PORTLAND POST CARD CO.

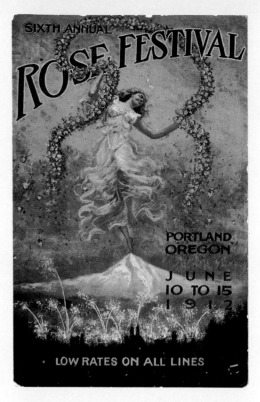

SIXTH ANNUAL
ROSE FESTIVAL
PORTLAND OREGON
JUNE 10 TO 15 1912
LOW RATES ON ALL LINES

For you a rose in Portland grows
TENTH ANNUAL
ROSE FESTIVAL
PORTLAND OREGON
JUNE 7 8 9 1916

FIFTH ANNUAL
Rose FESTIVAL
PORTLAND OREGON
JUNE 5 TO 10, 1911
LOW RATES ON ALL LINES
COPYRIGHTED BY PORTLAND POST CARD CO.

SEVENTH ANNUAL
ROSE FESTIVAL
PORTLAND OREGON
LOW RATES ON ALL LINES

EIGHTH ANNUAL
ROSE FESTIVAL
PORTLAND OREGON
JUNE 9 10 11 12 1914
FLORAL CONTESTS BALLOON RACES AQUATIC SPORTS FLORAL MILITARY
INDUSTRIAL ELECTRIC FRATERNAL PARADES BAND CONCERTS CARNIVAL

295. HOW PORTLAND'S FIRE DEPARTMENT DECORATES FOR THE ROSE FESTIVAL.

160:—A Prize Winning Float, Rose Festival, Portland. Ore.

Decorated Auto Rose Festival, Portland, Ore.

Fire Chief's Auto, Rose City Festival, Portland, Ore.

Decorated Auto, Rose Festival, Portland, Ore.

Greetings from "The Rose City"

Chinese Pheasant, Rose City Festival, Portland, Ore.

Queen of the Lily, Rose City Festival, Portland, Ore.

Resources of Oregon, Rose City Festival, Portland, Ore.

Rex Oregonus, Rose City Festival, Portland, Ore.

1913 Queen of the Roses

©1987 PAUL McGEHEE.

It is the place of Oregon that means the most. We must, first and foremost, cherish the place. All other good things will follow if we recognize the special beauty of Oregon first in all our planning; if we revere the magic; if we protect the quality.

Oregon has not been an over-eager lap-dog to the economic master. Oregon has been wary of smokestacks and suspicious of rattle and bang. Oregon has not camped, cup in hand, at anyone's affluent doorstep. Oregon has wanted industry only when that industry was willing to want what Oregon is.

Let us keep it that way. Let us have as much love for day-after-tomorrow as we have joy for today. Let's continue to learn the lessons and the legacies left us by the most fastidious land stewards in history — the Native Americans who lived in and worshipped at the Oregon shrine while our ancestors were still inhabiting cold, dark European caves.

Chief Sealth of the Duwamish Tribe said it best in a letter sent to the insouciant attention of President Franklin Pierce. The plea was ignored. "How can you buy or sell the sky — the warmth of the land? The idea is strange to us. Yet we do not own the freshness of the air or sparkle of the water. How can you buy them from us? Every part of this Earth is sacred to my people. Every shining pine needle, every sandy shore, every mist in the dark woods, every clearing and humming insect is holy in the memory and experience of my people. The air is precious to the Redman. For all things share the same breath — the beasts, the trees, the man."

That is a legacy we should swear to keep: Oregon, our Oregon — for all living things — now and in the generations to come.

—GOV. TOM MCCALL
June 3, 1971